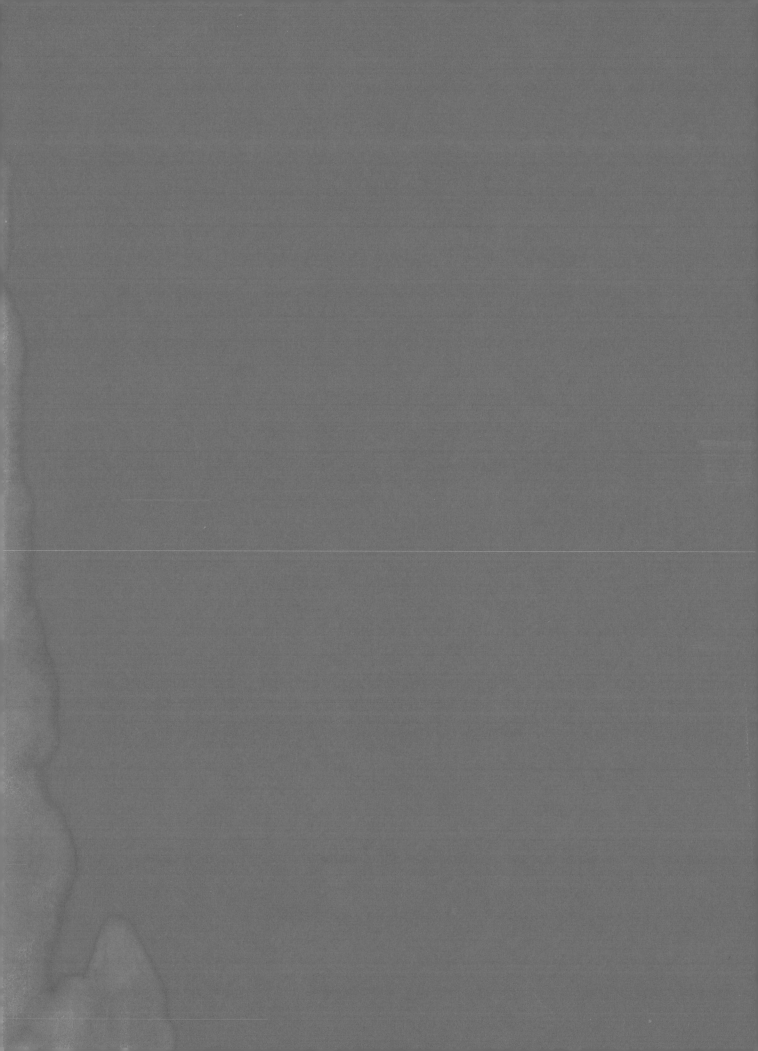

STOP DROP and ROLL

by Margery Cuyler

illustrated by Arthur Howard

Simon & Schuster Books for Young Readers
New York   London   Toronto   Sydney   Singapore

For my sister, Juliana
—M. C.

Special thanks to Lynn Parr's and Heidi Paisner's first-grade classes
at the Manhattan School of New York (P.S. 333) for their thoughtful comments.

SIMON & SCHUSTER BOOKS FOR YOUNG READERS
An imprint of Simon & Schuster Children's Publishing Division
1230 Avenue of the Americas, New York, New York 10020

With thanks to Julie Reynolds and the National Fire Protection Association
for their contributions to the making of this book.
Sparky® and Sparky's® Top 10 Fire Safety Tips for Kids are registered trademarks of the NFPA
© 2001, NFPA. All rights reserved. Used with permission.
National Fire Protection Association, 1 Batterymarch Park
P.O. Box 9101, Quincy, MA 02269-9101

Book design by Lily Malcolm and Mark Siegel
The text for this book is set in Garamond.
The illustrations are rendered in pen and ink, and watercolor.
Printed in the United States of America
2 4 6 8 10 9 7 5 3 1

Library of Congress Cataloging-in-Publication Data
Cuyler, Margery.
Stop, drop, and roll / Margery Cuyler;
[illustrated by] Arthur Howard.
p. cm.
Summary: Jessica, who worries about everything from her spelling
homework to remembering to fill her dog's water dish, learns that
fire safety begins with extinguishing her fears.
ISBN 0-689-84355-0
[1. Fire prevention–Fiction. 2. Safety–Fiction. 3. Worry–Fiction.]   I. Howard, Arthur, ill. II. Title.
PZ7. C997 St 2001
[E]–dc21
2001020803

Jessica was a worrier.
She worried morning, noon, and night.

She worried about her spelling homework,

and learning new
steps in ballet class,

and remembering to fill
her dog's water dish,

and waking up
in time for school.

But one Monday morning in October, Jessica's teacher gave her something new to worry about.

"It's Fire Prevention Week," explained Mr. Martin. "So for the next few days we're going to talk about fire safety."

"Uh-oh," groaned Jessica.

"And this Friday," Mr. Martin continued, "we've been asked to share what we've learned with the entire school."

"Oh, no," moaned Jessica.

"Let's begin with smoke alarms," said Mr. Martin. "Your homes should have them on every floor. Automatic fire sprinklers are a good idea, too."

Smoke alarms! Sprinklers!
Jessica had never seen either
in her house.

"Your families should also have escape plans in case of a
fire," said Mr. Martin. "And fire drills, so everyone knows
what to do."

Jessica chewed her pencil in
half. Escape plans! Now she
was really worried.

That night Jessica announced, "There is a big problem in this house. We have *no* smoke alarms and *no* sprinkler system. We don't even have an escape plan. If there was a fire, we'd be in trouble!"

Her mother puckered her forehead. "I remember buying smoke alarms. But I guess we never got around to installing them."

"And we talked about finding someone to put in sprinklers," added Dad. "But we're always too busy to make an appointment."

"And what about extra batteries for the alarms?" reminded Laura.

"Yeah," said Tom. "We need to keep more batteries around here."

Jessica twisted her napkin. She knew the real reason Tom wanted more batteries around. His birthday was in three days. He wanted batteries for his presents. But fire safety was more important than birthday toys, wasn't it?

"We've got to do something about this now!" warned Jessica.

"You're right," said Mom. "After dinner we'll make escape plans and find those smoke alarms."

"And tomorrow I'll get extra batteries and make arrangements for a sprinkler system," said Dad.

But Jessica still felt too worried to sleep.
She tossed and turned all night.

The next day Mr. Martin wrote some fire safety rules on the blackboard. "Never play with lighters or matches. Keep electric heaters at least three feet away from things that could burn.

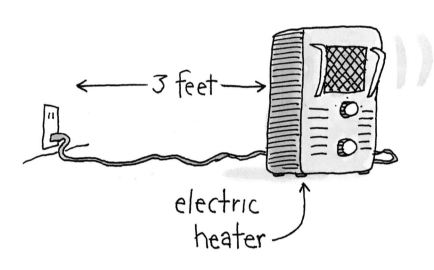

← 3 feet →

electric heater

"Keep extension cords away from doorways and from being pinched by furniture. A professional should check the chimneys and furnaces in your homes each year."

extension cord

professional

Blah. Blah. Blah. Mr. Martin went on and on until Jessica had to cover her ears. She'd never be able to remember so many things!

At dinner Jessica asked, "Have we ever had our chimney checked?"

"Yes," answered Dad. "When we bought the house."

"But Mr. Martin said it should be checked every year," said Jessica. "The furnace, too."

Dad sighed. "I'll put them on my list of things to do."

But that didn't stop Jessica from worrying.

She went through the entire house checking cords . . .

and smoke alarm batteries.

And she had another sleepless night imagining all the things that could go wrong.

On Wednesday, Mr. Martin had even more fire safety rules.

"Heat makes smoke rise. So if you're in a fire, you must crawl under the smoke where the air is cleaner. And when you reach a door, touch it. If it feels cool, it's safe to open."

Jessica tugged at a barrette. *What if the door felt warm? What should I do then?*

"If the door's warm," continued Mr. Martin, "don't open it. Find a window and call for help. Then wait for a firefighter to come and tell you what to do."

"And there's one more very important thing you need to know," said Mr. Martin. "If your clothes catch fire, stop what you're doing, drop to the ground, and roll over and over until you smother the flames."

Catch fire! Jessica had never been so worried in her life.

"Stop, drop, and roll," repeated Mr. Martin. "Let's all say it three times."

"Stop, drop, and roll. Stop, drop, and roll. Stop, drop, and roll," chanted the class.

All except Jessica. Her worries had twisted her tongue into a big knot.

When Jessica got home, she made her family have a fire drill.

Then she rechecked all the electrical cords, tested the batteries in all the smoke alarms, and made double sure that there were no matches lying around.

Afterward Jessica felt a little better, but she still couldn't get Mr. Martin's words from class right.

"Stop, slop, and troll. Mop, pop, and bowl." The harder Jessica tried, the worse she did. But she went to sleep feeling a little better. At least she knew what to do if there was a fire during the night.

Then, on Thursday, disaster struck. Mr. Martin asked Jessica to demonstrate "Stop, drop, and roll" at the assembly the next day.

Why me? thought Jessica.

On the bus home she tried to practice the words—"Stop, flop, and roll? Flop, mop, and stroll? Stop, pop, and hole?"—but they kept coming out wrong.

Jessica was so worried about the assembly that she couldn't even enjoy Tom's birthday party.

"Stop, drop, and mole. Slop, drop, and hole. Plop, mop, and stroll," she muttered to herself.

Because of all her muttering, she didn't even notice when Mom brought in the cake. It had seven big candles on it. Six were for Tom's sixth birthday and one was for him to wish on.

And just as Tom leaned over to blow them out,
Jessica looked up and saw fire.

"STOP, DROP, AND ROLL!" she screamed.

Immediately Tom stopped blowing and
dropped to the floor . . .

. . . but before he rolled, Jessica saw that Tom wasn't on fire at all.

Jessica's worries had gotten the best of her. She was so embarrassed!

"False alarm!" said Dad.

"Phew!" said Mom. "You gave me quite a scare."

"I'm sorry," said Jessica. "But I thought—"

"You thought quickly!" interrupted Dad. "That's good, because it's better to be safe than sorry."

"Besides," added Laura, "you finally said it right!"

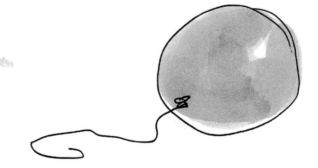

And that was the truth. Jessica *had* said the words right. And now that she had, she was confident she'd never forget any of the fire safety rules she had learned that week.

And you know what? She never did.